THE

CORRUPTION OF ESTABLISHED TRUTH

AND

RESPONSIBILITY OF EDUCATED MEN.

AN ADDRESS

DELIVERED BEFORE THE ALUMNI OF THE UNIVERSITY OF MICHIGAN,

JUNE 27, 1856.

BY REV. N. WEST, JR.
Of Cincinnati, Ohio.

[PUBLISHED BY REQUEST.]

"*Scientia nihil aliud est quam veritatis imago.*"

DETROIT:
FREE PRESS BOOK AND JOB STEAM PRINTING ESTABLISHMENT.
1856.

ADDRESS.

GENTLEMEN OF THE ALUMNI:

Obedient to a venerated custom, we have turned aside from the various professions and pursuits of life to mingle, for a short time, our mutual congratulations, and renew the familiar intimacies we were wont to cherish in former days. It is well if, notwithstanding the toils of arduous duty, the vicissitudes of prosperous or adverse providence, and all the transitions of our respective histories, we yet entertain for our "*Alma Mater*" that devotion and enthusiasm we once felt for her in years gone by. Better still will it be, if, as returning to complete the circle of our wanderings at her door, and receive her cordial welcome, she finds us such as she desired us to be when our feet left her threshold and our hearts carried away her word of parting; sons worthy of her anxious care; stewards diligent in the improvement of her munificent gifts, an honor to her name, a credit to ourselves and a blessing to the world!

The great mission upon which we were sent, and for the successful accomplishment of which we were furnished with a thorough, though incipient, intellectual and moral training, was to promote the welfare of our fellow men, by standing forth as the champions of truth against error, in whatever sphere of effort, and seeking by means of the truth to eliminate a *life* of usefulness and a result of practical good from all with whom we came in contact. This was our mission. To this one end all our running, all our practice, all our discipline, in the curriculum of collegiate instruction, was religiously directed. We studied nothing in the classics, nothing in the mathematics, nothing in ethics, history, logic or rhetoric, mastered nothing in the evidences of Christianity, in philosophy, literature, art or science, heard no voice of prayer, no song of praise, no word of sacred wisdom, received no reproof, partook of no advice, felt no generous impulse, and were urged to no laudable ambition, which had not this one end and aim in view, the fitting of us to discharge our duty to our fellow men.

The occasion which has called us together, even the hailed recurrence of the time when we issued forth in prosecution of this work, to grapple with the activities of an untried contest, suggests a theme, the consideration of which claims alike the attention of the *patriot*, the *scholar* and the *christian* It is THE PRESENT CORRUPTION OF ESTABLISHED TRUTH, AND THE PRESENT RESPONSIBILITY OF EDUCATED MEN.

In seeking for a definition of truth, we do not content ourselves simply with an inquiry into the agreement or non-agreement of our verbal expressions, either with our conceptions, convictions, or objects of real existence. This were to terminate the inquiry upon words. But we seek to ascertain what that is which lies behind the expressions, as a substance behind a sign, and of which these expressions, in whatever department of learning, are only the articulate announcements. Is there, in the universe, such a thing as truth, and is it well established? Does it exist *out* of the mind, as well as *in* the mind? Is it immutable and eternal, or does it depend upon the ever-changing and capricious intellect of man? These are questions, in reference to which there has been a contest both severe and protracted. Philosophers have undertaken to show that, although there is indeed such a thing as truth in the world, yet in the last analysis of its character it is found to be but a representation of the mind to itself; that it is something devoid of objectivity; that, were the mind destroyed, truth would be destroyed also; that the mind sees only what itself originates, nothing more, nothing less; that truth is the subjective intelligence objectified, or the product of reason projected upon the plane of consciousness; in other words, the mind mirrored to itself so that percipient and perceived are identical, just as a man standing before a mirror beholds only himself. Like Daphnis, the beautiful shepherd whom Virgil celebrates, and who caught a sight of his own image in the water, as one day he stood by the shore of the sea when the winds were still,

> "Nuper me in litore vidi,
> Cum placidum ventis staret mare;"

so these philosophers, in their contemplative moods, have looked into the calm unrippled sea of consciousness, and beholding there the image of themselves, have declared it to be the only truth, existence. Or, like Narcissus, sung by Ovid, who came to slake his thirst at a silver spring, into which no branch of a tree had ever fallen, and where no shepherd or flock had ever been, and there beheld in the glassy fountain a form of youthfulness and naked beauty, so these philosophers coming to the mirror of consciousness, a mirror discovered by Des Cartes in the last half of the seventeenth century, and into which none before had ever taken the trouble to look intently, became enraptured with the visions of beauty there seen, and publishing to the world the unsubstantial idealities of their own imaginative brain, the "*Rem sine corpore*," and the "*Corpus quod umbra est*" of the self-smitten lover, gave out that the "*me*" and the "*not-me*," the subject and object, were "*all-one*," and the only real truth. We are affirmed to be the victims of a complete delusion, according this very delusive theory, if we think we either see or believe anything which we ourselves have not originated, and which we ourselves already are not. To teach that truth, at any time, is other and different from what we imagine, construct, or represent it to be, or that there is any greater measure of existence than our own mental capacity, or that the horizon of our knowledge must be less at all times, than the domain of our faith, is a philosophical heresy, and obnoxious to the anger of the higher speculative criticism.

In opposition to this, we hold that in the very nature of the case, man can never be other than himself, neither can his capacity to know be the measure of existence, neither is he perfect in his present condition. He cannot, therefore, be *all*, neither can he be *more* than he is, neither can his knowledge be commensurate with what he is bound to believe, nor can the image of himself be the standard of truth. Truth has an existence *out* of the individual mind, as well as in it, pure, absolute, indefectible. It is immutable in its nature, divine in its origin, eternal in its history. Existing in all the forms of organic life and inorganic nature, being the *toute ensemble* of facts and relations in the heavens above, earth beneath, and waters under the earth, pervading all departments of knowledge, energizing through all things, human and divine, according to its unchanging principles and laws, it is evermore the *teacher* and not the child of man. Apprehended by the natural intelligence, as an object is seen by the natural eye, or grasped by the natural hand, it cannot be that which the mind *originates*, but only that which it seeks. It is the pearl of great price in all the divisions of human and divine science, the which, when a man finds, he parts with all his meaner merchandise, to buy. Celestial in its birth and synonymous with light, it yet resides in all the provinces where literature, philosophy, art, science, and religion take their origin, is that after which we are all in pursuit, and without which we are never satisfied. This truth, gentlemen, misapprehended, misconceived, misapplied, by the professed explorers and expounders of it, during the last half century, and even now, has been subjected, in consequence thereof, to an illegitimate expression and false presentation upon the pages of the literature of the age. Speculatively, practically, scientifically, and religiously, it has been corrupted, and to-day lifts up its voice in protest against the metamorphosis. There is not a department of human or divine knowledge that is free from the perversion. The fountains of literature are poisoned, and the streams are pestilential. Society drinks of the turbid waters, sulphurous and brackish, like those of the Dead Sea, only to experience their painful results. That error and almost universal unbelief which have rolled their surging waves across the continents and islands of the old world, dash themselves to-day against the shores, the cities, and towns, of the New.

Holding ourselves responsible for what we are about to utter, we say that the cause of this wide-spread corruption of established truth is not so difficult to be ascertained, as many suppose. It is palpable to any one, who, casting his eyes over the fields of literature in our own age, and comparing them with the same fields of a former age, has discernment sufficient to mark the peculiarity of difference between the two, and diligence enough to trace it through all its varied ramifications. There is but one cause for the universal unbelief, in the higher walks of life, during the last half century; one cause for all the perversions of scientific and religious truth; one cause for all the mental restlessness of society; one cause for all the bewitchment and enchantment of the studious intellect; one cause for all the false philosophy, false divinity, and false humanity of the present era. That cause finds its appropriate expression in one word, and that word is "DEVELOPMENT." Like a mighty serpent, or boa-constrictor, it has wormed itself through, coiled itself round, and spread its slime over, all the departments of human investigation.

We hazard nothing in attributing so powerful an influence to *one* idea, for how many times has one idea revolutionized the world and all learning! With one idea, Copernicus and Galileo demolished the system of Ptolemy and Eudoxus, and opened a new era in astronomy; with one idea, Newton gave law to the universe; by one idea, the theory of self-consciousness, Des Cartes became the father of modern metaphysics; by one idea, that of induction, Bacon redeemed philosophy from the bondage of mediœval authority; by one idea, the distinction between reason and understanding, Kant agitated all speculative science to the centre; by one idea, that of a three-fold system of existence unfolded by Dialectic Method, Hegel towered above all his predecessors, and drew Germany in captivity to his feet. And so this one idea of development, misconceived, distorted, misapplied and misrepresented by the savants of science, has spread its contagious influence over every acre of intellectual territory hitherto explored by man, poisoned the whole literature of the last half century, and produced as its result the universal skepticism, both scientific and religious, of the present age. Viewed in whatever light, whether as teaching that all things are derived from an infusorial point; or that there is but one primitive germ for all possible variations, and that no variation is impossible; or that all organic germs are identical; or that in the line of organic progress there is a veritable transmutation of the species, a passing over of one thing into something other and different from itself; or that all superior forms of existence, celestial or terrestrial, animate or inanimate, have been pushed out and pushed up into the higher from the lower, by inherent forces; or that whatever is best in the universe, in history, morals, science or religion, is but an organic growth, an "*Aufhebung*," of what is worst—viewed, we say, in whatever light, it has yielded a luxuriant harvest of noxious weeds in all the departments of learning. The two modes of its pushing, or its two forms of embryotic hypothesis and transmutation theory, like the two horns of the little Beast in the Apocalypse, betray its terrene origin and its destructive propensities.

In adducing the evidence of our theme, that the misapprehended and misapplied idea of development has been the real cause of the wide-spread corruption of religious and scientific truth, we are admonished to be brief because the field is immense. And *first*, in the territory of the Natural Sciences, to mention only Botany, Zoology, Astronomy and Geology, this evidence is complete. The student of these departments cannot be ignorant of the names of Goethe, Oken,

Meckel, Geoffrey St. Hilaire, La Marck, Herschell, La Place, and their cotemporaries, all eminent men and leaving the impress of their genius upon their varied departments of study. To the German poet belongs the credit of propounding the doctrine of the metamorphosis of plants. To Oken, as he stumbled over the Hartz mountains, where ghosts are said to be numerous, the honor of resuscitating the wild and defunct theory of De Maillet, that all vegetation is from the sea, the primordial source of all life, so that the majestic oaks of the forest, the luxuriant fruit-trees of the orchard, and the fragrant flowers of the garden, were developed by a process altogether unique, from kelp-weed, tangle and willows, just as these in turn had come from marine-grass, reeds and flags. To St. Hilaire and La Marck, the former of whom was entrusted with the presidency of the Zoological Museum, in Paris, belongs the merit of disputing the doctrine of Cuvier, and maintaining the hypothesis that there is but one type from which all the variations of the animal kingdom are unfolded, according to organic law; so that the polype, the mollusc, and the man, are reducible to the same primitive form. According to this theory, advocated by the author of the "Vestiges of Creation," man is pre-eminently favored with an exalted position at the apex of the zoological pyramid, because he contains within his own organization the sum total of all the special structures below him. Still more, he is honored with *a blood relationship*, on this very account, to all that exists beneath him, the ape, the elephant, and the mouse alike, so that Cuvier was but the expansion of an Ourang Outang, and St. Hilaire and Lamarck only the cynosures in their own menagerie, organically pushed out and up, by a special inherent conatus, from the lower forms of the tadpole, the frog, and the monkey. These same philosophers, and their coadjutors, turning to the Geological field, applied the same theory to the fossiliferous strata of the earth, contending that existing species sprang from extinct forms, and insisting that the proof of actual transmutation was found registered in the stony record of the past. The theory of successive creations was ignored, and superposition of strata held to be evidence of parental relation. True, indeed, it was admitted that the primitive germs or infusorial points were *not to be discovered,(!)* but then, notwithstanding this, the lowest specimens of extinct forms, buried in the lowest strata, were the real progenitors of all that now moves on the land, swims in the sea, or floats in the air. In astronomy, the speculations of the elder Herschell led to the Nebular hypothesis of La Place, so that the popular cosmogony was based upon the theory of a primitive fire-mist or vapor, out of which the stars, planets, suns, and worlds of the universe, were gradually evolved. In every one of these departments of investigation, a personal God was ruled out of the question, the doctrine of providence denied, and final causes ignored. Thus it was that a complete system of infidelity fastened itself upon the sciences, by the almost simultaneous application of the development theory to all, and that the talent and genius of the age engaged in a scientific crusade against, not only theistic truth, but also against the oracles of revelation.

Again, in the region of the higher metaphysics, the same idea has corrupted all the legitimate speculations of philosophy. And here we enter a field which, however much we may affect to despise, and however much regard as beyond the comprehension of the people, is yet more potent and dangerous against the truth, because more subtle and specious. What boots it the philosopher whether the people can follow him in his abstract theorizings and mazy wanderings, provided only the *results* of his labors are accepted? Newton was satisfied that the world should believe the laws he demonstrated, without being able to read his Principia. La Place was satisfied that his theory of the universe should be regarded as true, without the world's being able to read his Mecanique Celeste. Similarly, Kant, Fichte, Schelling, and Hegel, would have been gratified that the results of their philosophy should be accepted by the people, even though their processes were scarcely understood. On this point we need fear. History assures us that no matter how wild the vagary may be, it will always find abundant neophytes to advocate its absurdities. There is a continual longing in unsettled minds for something newer, an Athenian-like thirst for "τὶ καινότερον," ever ready to study, imbibe, and print the errors it has not the power or ingenuity to originate; and there is an equal thirst in the multitude to receive whatever is thus provided, whether in the pamphlet, the duodecimo, or the pouplar lecture.

In higher metaphysics the *absolute idea* corresponds to the infusorial point, or primitive germ, in the Natural sciences. It is from this the universe is evolved by necessary organic development. The thought here is stupendous in its erratic grandeur. All other developments, in all other sciences, when compared with this, are but as tapers to the sun, or drops to the ocean. This one soars above all, embraces all, is the parent of all. Botany, Zoology, Astronomy, Geology, and all other sciences, are but simple modes according to which the absolute proceeds in majesty and living power. Politics, philosophy, religion and revolution, are but the spontaneous breathings, the irrepressible pulsations of this mighty movement, each a special conatus of the monster-ideal-world-germ, or primitive universe-embryo, from which all things come. This embryo is called God! History is his enacted life under the two conditions of Eternity and Infinity. This germ becomes conscious of its own existence, only in the consciousness of man, and the instincts of brutes. Everything that exists is God. From Him all existence is developed—rocks, streams, trees, birds, beasts, fishes and men. He is all things, and all things are Him. Pantheists, in beginning their philosophy, can claim, at least, the merit of Damœtas in beginning his song.

"Ab Jove principium, Musœ; Jovis omnia plena."

It is interesting to observe the progress of the corruption of philosophy and its termination in this doctrine of the Absolute. Briefly, Des Cartes had defined a *substance* to be that which exists independently of all things. Spinoza accepted the definition and built upon it a system of material pantheiom, making God to be the only substance, having the two attributes of thought and extension. Malebranche followed with the declaration that we have an immediate vision of God in all things. Leibnitz constructed his monadology, for the purpose of harmonizing speculative difficulties, and taught that one monad was the parent of all the rest, and that monad was God. Kant separated the thinking "*me*" from the external world, and left it for his successors to explain the relation between them. Fichte, protesting, against the separation, united both, and reduced everything to the subjective side, to the "*me*," of which all things were the effect. This was too much, for God, on this scheme, was destroyed. The charge of Atheism forced the philosopher to retract, and reinstate God, making the "*me*," however, His image. Schelling undertook to explain the relation between the two, which Fichte had abandoned, by finding in the principle of identity the required unity of both. Hegel, stepped in and declared that the objective was nothing by itself, nor the subjective anything by itself, neither both together, but that reality was to be found alone in the *relation* between them, that this was the only existence. Thus it was that the Absolute, the abstraction of Nothing, became the philosophical embryo or primitive germ of all things, the source of all the universe. Spinoza had made God to be simply an animated geological conglomerate. This huge specimen is next put into the crucible of the higher criticism, there to seethe, hiss and simmer, until it comes to a double-bubble-bubble,—Fichte looking until he sees the "*me*" in it, his own image,—Schelling looking until he sees the "*me*" and the "*not-me*," all one, himself and the universe just alike, and, last of all, Hegel, the ὕπατυ of the grand trio of metaphysical speculators, remaining until the substance is sublimated away into the abstract idea of Nothing, the essence of all existence, and exclaiming with uplifted hands *Seyn ist Nichts*; the marvelous equation at the threshold of all his philosophy!

Thus it was, by a vain attempt to construct the universe, a priori, and to bridge the gulf between the ideal and the real, that all Europe was flooded with a spring tide of infidelity, the waves of which have not yet subsided, and the violence of which has propelled it to our own shores!

Time forbids me, gentlemen, to dwell long upon the havoc made in the Christian field, by the application of this one idea of development, at one time in one form, at another time in another. Yet a word of illustration may be allowed here also in proof of our theme. In all ages, the effect of philosophy upon revealed religion has been that of subversion and not of edification. Biblical truth has been corrupted by every metaphysical *system*, that of Sir William Hamilton, so far as it goes, not excepted. Platonism prevailed among the church Fathers and Aristotelianism among the schoolmen. After the reformation, error again began its invasions. First the Wolfian, then the Kantian, then the Schellingian, and last of all the Hegelian metaphysics, were applied to Christianity, in theological chairs, and expounded from sacred pulpits. The result has been the denial of the inspiration of the scriptures in any Biblical sense, and the substitution of a genius-theory, according to which all the religious truths of the Bible are but the result of self-elevation. Of course the divine authority of the Scriptures is ruled out as a superstition. The rationalism of Kant, the intuitionalism of Schelling, the subjectiveism of Fichte, and the dialectic method of Hegel, all find here a common centre of union. Miracles are pronounced to be impossible, by a foregone conclusion, and the Biblical ones are explained as myths, fabulous representations of an uncivilized age and people. The Greeks, Romans, Persians, Egyptians and Scandinavians had myths in their early history; why should not the Hebrews? Moses, Elias, Abraham and Jesus, are paralleled with Theseus, Hercules, Jupiter, and Bacchus! If Ormusd and Odin are not historical, then neither are Adam and Noah. Prophecy, once ridiculed as a post-vaticination, is kindly relieved from this reproach and declared to be a simple reference to events existing at the time of its utterance, and its application to the Messiah but a distorted mode of thinking, on the part of His Jewish followers! The man of Nazareth is held to be only a personified idea!

In like manner, Christianity itself is regarded only as a phase of the Absolute religion,—a religion developed, by one set of philosophers, from the Absolute idea, and by another, from the lowest forms of Fetichism. This last hypothesis has for its most gifted advocate the author of the Positive Philosophy. Yet, not content to take Hegel on the one hand, or Auguste Comte on the other, a transit has been made into the field of Natural Science for the purpose of applying the two-fold form of development, there illustrated, to Christianity and the church. Thus, all the corruptions of the church during the first four centuries, and the middle ages have been, on the embryotic principle, explained as necessary growths from the Apostolic germ. Or, if it is found that there are many developments in the history of the church, the seminal elements of which cannot be discovered in Apostolic Christianity, then the transmutation theory is introduced to account for the change, and relieve us from further trouble. Somehow or other, there was a wonderful inherent tendency to progressive improvement about the year A. D., 606, and the felt wants of the church gave rise to a special conatus or effort. True, it was not a growth in grace that was desired, yet still there was a desire for a growth. And just as the special conatus of a globule of jelly produced, for it, hands and mouth, and feet, so that it passed over to be a frog, and just as the special conatus for swimming formed for the frog, fins and tail, so that it passed over to be a shark, just so the special conatus of pure Apostolic Christianity for becoming an ecclesiastico-political despotism formed for it all the attributes of such a system, *and thus it passed over to Popery!* Such, gentlemen, is the theory as applied to the church. Everything of corruption, by wicked men, in it and about it, is held to be a regular organic development. We are not allowed to step behind, or overleap the boundaries of a mixed historical evolution of doctrine, practice or worship, no matter how corrupted, to seek for pure truth in the original Scriptures. The stream of development bears us on, and we must keep in the current. Historians tell us there are *two* factors in history, God and man; but there is a Satanic *third* of no small potency and will!

It would require a volume, many volumes, to set forth in proper order and bearing, the truths which have been corrupted, sacrificed, and denied, by the application of this one idea of development. The imperfect glance we have taken at only three general departments of learning, viz: The Natural Sciences, Metaphysics, and Religion, suffices to show how fearful the havoc has been. The distinction between a personal God and His works is obliterated,—the doctrine of a primitive creation denied—the Creator, by necessity, excluded from the world—providential interposition ruled out as a figment and folly—and final causes rejected as a dream of superstition. The authority of an independent Will and Power, controlling the universe has been exchanged for the government of Blind Fate, energizing mechanically according to the rules of geometrical action, in every department, and baptized with the name of Eternal Law. The Bible is said to be the work of man, or of God only in so far as God and man are one. Its miracles are declared to be myths, its prophecies metaphors, its histories delusions, its Messiah a fabled incarnation, yea, the tenth avatar of Vishnu! Fetichism, Brahmism, Ssufism, Judaism, Christianity, Popery, Mohammedism, Mormonism, and Infidelity, all are phases of the one same Absolute religion. The modern corruptions of Christianity are only legitimate outgrowths from itself. The doctrine of the original perfection of all things, has been removed to give place to that of original imperfection, and the theory of the permanence of the species ignored for that of its transmutation. Man, once made in the likeness of Jehovah, and announced as the last, the highest effort of creative skill and wisdom, is called upon by modern science to look at his picture, on the one hand, in the wild barbarian, the uncombed Caffre of the jungle, and on the other, to find his traditional ancestor in an infusorial point, or globule of jelly, animated by electricity; and tracing his pedigree through the rocky pages of his family register, to discover there among his relations a Megatherium of the later Pliocene, ro an Ichthyosaaurus of the Upper Secondary! Passing into the field of metaphysics, he learns the further lesson that he is God! all that exists being only himself developed, that he is the Eternal Spider, weaving from his own substance the entire tissue of the universe, and by a process of subsumption, gathering it up again; or, to use another figure of the Hindoo system, he is the Sun from which all rays, the Ocean from which all waves, proceed. Thus, he becomes his own father, his own brother, his own son, and all the rest of the family included;—the "*me*" and the "*not me*," all one; an independent mighty individual, the sum total of everything, afraid of no one, above, beneath, or around him, but "*monarch of all he surveys.*"

"The form and the substance, the what and the why,
The when and the where, the low and the high;
The inside and outside, the earth and the sky,
All souls and all bodies,—I, I, itself I."

What to denominate such a system, it is difficult to tell. Yet unquestionably it has a kinsman relationship to that Atheistic philosophy of the ancients so admirably described by the gifter Cudworth,—"a monster, big-swoln with a puffy show of wisdom, which, though he struts and talks so gigantically, and marches with such a kind of stately philosophic grandeur, yet is indeed but like the giant Orgoglio in our English poet, a mere empty bladder, blown up with vain conceit, an Empusa, phantasm, or spectre, the offspring of night and darkness, of nonsense and contradiction.!"

We shall not stop to prove to you, gentlemen, that this misconceived and misapplied idea of development has resulted in the *paganization* of human learning. It is a sad fact to know that what is so boastfully and magniloquently held up to be the advance of science, in modern times, proves, upon a patient and toilsome investigation, to be but the retrogression of science. The whole past has been exhumed, and brought forward, by the active spirit of the last fifty years. There is nothing in the essential theories of St. Hilaire, La March, Oken, La Place, Fichte, Hegel, Comte, or the author of the Vestiges of Creation, which cannot be found in Anaximander, Xenophanes, Epicurus and Democritus, which cannot be read in Plato, Cicero, Lucretius, Persius, and Virgil. To adduce but one instance, for the sake of illustration: Xenophanes asserted that "if oxen and lions had hands and fingers, and could produce works like men, oxen would represent their gods *like* oxen, and lions their gods *like* lions, and assign them the sort of form themselves possess. Feuerbach, a German pantheist, published in the year A. D., 1840, these words:—"If God were an object to a *bird*, he would be a *winged* being; the bird knows nothing higher, nothing more blissful than the winged condition." Where, gentlemen, is the difference in the mighty principle of error which lies at the foundation of the philosophy of these two men? One of them teaches, one thousand eight hundred and forty years *after* Christ, just what the other taught five hundred and thirty years *before* Christ, and this doctrine has been, in our day, the reigning metaphysics of Europe! Has philosophy advanced, then, during the two thousand three hundred years of her activity? Rather, has not Paganism received a resurrection at the hand of modern scholars? The remark of Voltaire, ribald and jesting as it was, yet contains a truth which every student can see, as soon as it is announced;—"Philosophy is the inverse reading of the passage 'God made man in His own image;' *man returns God the compliment!*"

But, perhaps, you are ready to ask, gentleman, how it is that this theory of development, so productive of evil, has become so universally received, and so supremely successful? how, notwithstanding the discoveries made by the telescope of Lord Rosse, the argument furnished by the indefatigable Hugh Miller, from the Star-Scale of Stromness, and the merciless criticisms of such a man as Sir William Hamilton, it yet prevails, and seems to gather strength in many of the circles of science? Our answer is, just because there *are* elements, vital germs of undeniable truth in it, giving to it all its power, but without which it would shrink, wither, and die, in a day! There *is* truth in the doctrine of the "Unity of Organic Composition," propounded by St. Hilaire,—truth in the doctrine of a "Dialectic Method," or progressive rythm of all being, propounded by Hegel,—truth in the doctrine of a "Church-Development," propounded by a Mœhler, a Bauer, a Newman, a Nevin,—and truth even in the Positive Philosophy. The properties and criteria of a true development, could be culled very readily, either by special extracts or just inferences, from the writings of all these authors. But, yet, the truth here found, as it lies in their pages, and is connected with their schemes, is so distorted, so misapprehended, so corrupted, and so grossly misapplied to the subject in hand, and to the facts of the case, that positive error is the result. "*Corruptio optimi pessima*,"—the corruption of the best is the worst corruption—finds here its clearest illustration. The truth of God is "changed into a lie," and yet because of the very semblance of truth which the theory puts on, and the elements of truth to which it points, it conciliates success. The man who, like the German idealists, and Cousin their trumpet, fails to give prominence in his system to the distinction between the *act of reason* apprehending truth, and the *truth apprehended*, however much he may speak of the distinction, and contemplates only the co-residence of truth and reason in the same mind, will soon transfer to reason the properties of impersonality and eternity which alone belong to truth, and find himself in a pantheistic circle from which he cannot escape. Every thing must come from the "*me*." Man will be God, and from this point development must proceed. Now, there are elements of truth even here, but so misapplied that error only is the result. And the man who, like St. Hilaire, beholds only organic unity in all things, but beholds not organic diversity, and both as facts of a primitive creation, neither allows in the line of progress the intervention of creative power, but exalts his own partial idea into equivalency with the Supreme Plan, cannot fail to propound a theory which, however plausible it may be, will yet only produce the fruits of error. Truth, indeed, it will contain, and this will give it life, and ensure it success for a time; and the dazzling grandeur of teeming millions of animated beings, deploying into line according to a fixed law of development, and marching onward and upward to higher forms, like the steady movement of an issuing host, will spread such a scene of magnificence before the ardent imagination, as may well bewilder and enchant the profoundest minds. But it would only be an illustration of the ridiculousness of the theory, should any one, thus viewing this host, apply to a regiment of its cavalry the doctrine that *superposition proves parental relation*, and argue that the horses were the fathers of the riders, the higher a development from the lower, and both organically one, mythological Centaurs, like those who dwelt on the summits of Pelion and Thessaly, or fanciful monsters, like that depicted in the opening of the Ars Poetica,—the compound of a horse, a woman, a bird, and a fish! Theologians make no better showing when they apply this perverted theory to Christianity and the church.

And now, gentlemen, what is the responsibility of the educated man in view of the wide-spread corruption of religious and scientific truth? Viewed in the light of its practical bearing upon the individual, the family, the church, the state, and upon all the beneficent institutions of society, can it be a matter of small consequence that such a theory as the one we have alluded to, be encouraged and espoused? Witness its application to all the departments of learning, and its arrogant pretension that nothing is unquestionably established but itself. Consider the historical fruits of that application, as they have matured in the kingdoms of Insular and Continental Europe,—how, from the boughs of this mystical Upas, all-blasting in its nature, have proceeded Communism, Socialism, Spiritualism, Materialism, Blasphemy, Revolution, and Unbelief, in their direst forms; how the ties of domestic life have been sundered, the fountains of social happiness poisoned, the elements of political stability dissolved, and the eternal principles of religion and virtue ignored! At work, already in the class-room of the College and University, in the chairs of Theology, in the pulpits of churches, lauded by the press, and supported by infidel coteries throughout the land, it bids fair to take root in the intellectual soil of our own country. Is the responsibility, then, light, is the obligation trivial, that rests upon the shoulders of the home-trained graduates of the nation, to be the conservators of whatever is good and true? None weightier ever fell upon the shoulders of any. No victory more brilliant than that which one day will crown the fortunes of those who battle manfully for the truth, ever perched upon the banners and standards of the past. The foe is not to be despised, for it is one of a Trio of unclean spirits sent forth from the mouth of the Dragon who more than ever appears as an "angel of light!" It is the Mimic and Ape of the Most High in His plans and purposes, and speaks boastingly of a social and political Millennium. Unlike the scepticism of the last century, which was coarse and vulgar, this is fine and attractive. It rallies to its aid all the accomplishments of science and learning, is crested with genius, arrays itself in the garb of truth, and pours in the witchery of eloquence and enchantment of song.

The mode, gentlemen, of combatting this enemy, is simple and plain. The strongest weapons of attack and defence, are, as they ever have been, the oracles of divine wisdom, in so far as they bear upon the error to be destroyed. And here we have an abundant equipment, for the truth is ready to our hand. We have only to open our eyes in order to see it. There is indeed a true development theory, built upon a true law of development, an eternal theory pervaded by an eternal law, a mighty plan, a pattern-idea, ever present in all the variations of existence, causing us to wonder at the simplicity of its design, the adaptation of its means, and the magnificence of its execution. Obvious amid all its manifold complications, beautiful in the regularity of its movements, and harmonious with itself throughout the departments of Nature, Revelation, and History, each illustrating, confirming, and interpenetrating the other, it challenges our admiration because of its perfection, and wins our assent because of its truth. It meets the false theory of perverted science, by proclaiming that its introduction into the universe was heralded by the miracle of a primitive creation;—not the creation simply of a common embryo, germ, or infusorial point, in which the characteristics of future organizations were potentially concealed, but the creation in maturity of each distinct kind by itself, from which, as a point of beginning, all things were to proceed. The universal law for all life was clearly announced in the first institution of the organic kingdom. Every living thing was created, each "*after its kind*," and each having "*its seed in itself.*" Here was the sublime, yet simple plan, the static and dynamic principles of the Cosmos inseparably blended together, teaching the impossibility of the last without the presence of the first, and that whatever is developed must be *identical with itself* throughout the entire line of its progress, the oak producing the acorn, the acorn the oak, the man the child, the child the man, down to the latest generations,—all departments of organic life, constructed on the seminal plan, any deviation from which would only be a resultant monstrosity. The development was to be, not of one thing from another, but each from itself.

Parallel with this, another law is plainly discoverable, equally grand as the first, the intervention of creative power, by successive acts, during the progress of the plan. New forms are seen to arise, period after period, not according to a transmutation hypothesis, but according to the direct intervention, of creative power the original and previous principles ever being carried forward in the line of advance; interruptions also where it pleased the Creator to make them, and mysterious combinations to show forth His wisdom and goodness. One general plan, one general order, everywhere seen in the various sections of organized existence, modified, indeed, to suit the design of the skillful Architect, yet no confounding of a first with a second creation, nor of a first with a second development. There were, indeed, to be "diversities of operations" in the natural as well as in the spiritual kingdom, but then, in the one as in the other, "the same God who worketh all in all," was to appear conspicuous. Men were not to be sent fig-hunting in thistle-ground, nor grape-gathering in a thorn-brake. The fig-tree was not to bear olive-berries, neither a vine figs. The physiologist and anatomist were to look in vain for an example where any race had unfolded itself into another and a different one. Vegetation was not to assume the aspect of the brute creation, neither was the brute to obtrude itself into the form of humanity. External, and other, causes might, indeed, interfere to warp the development out of its true growth, for a time, but yet so imperative was the original law that the legitimate development *must* recur, as soon as these disturbing influences should be removed. The entire universe was to march forward, under the control of a superintending providence, not according to the formula of the purblind philosopher, but according to the development of a magnificent plan, worthy of God, even to the whole extent of its primitive creations, its established laws, and successive interventions.

Such is an outline of a true theory. Such is the one for which we are ever to contend. The application of such a theory to all departments of learning will be accompanied with the happiest results.—Christianity will never be referred to as a form of Fetichism, or regarded as the germ of a rationalistic creed. Biblical truth will ever remain identical with itself while it seeks a higher development in the spiritual life of the soul, and the church. Philosophy, constructing itself upon the primary beliefs of the human mind, will never fabricate a psychology to suit an a priori hypothesis, nor overlook the already recorded facts of consciousness. Natural science will no longer indulge the license of imaginative poets and painters, by coupling serpents with birds, and lambs with tigers, but following the *divine* law of identity in development, "first the blade, then the ear, after that the full corn in the ear," will utter its formula in the words of the Roman bard, admirable and true,

> "Servetur ad imum
> Qualis ab incœpto processerit, et sibi constet."

Gentlemen of the Alumni :

Were it not for the Bible, our argument would be, comparatively speaking, of small moment. But, admitting the Bible to be a divine revelation, the argument assumes proportions of importance it is impossible to measure. That divine Book is "the transcript of the divine will, the portrait of the divine character, the charter of human rights, the guide of human hope, the comforter of the human heart and counsellor of human ignorance." It is for *its* truth, all other truth has value. Every effort in the discovery, illustration, and confirmation of scientific truth is an effort in behalf of a divine revelation. Every perversion and corruption of scientific truth, is a perversion of *it*, for in *it* are latent all the seeds of human knowledge. The responsibility, then, of the educated man is the mightiest in its discharge, either for happiness or misery. The call for united effort on the part of the lovers of truth, is to-day, the loudest that has ever been made. The battle-field is wide, and embraces the whole territory of human investigation. The remark of Hugh Miller, that "it is in the departments of physics, not metaphysics, that the greater minds of the age are engaged," and that the contest for Bible truth is "to be fought on the field of physical science," is one-sided and partial. This contest cannot be limited, principally or chiefly, to such a sphere. Metaphysical science is yet in the field, and powerfully too. Though Hume, and Kant, and Fichte, and Hegel, are dead, still they live in their works, and successors, and speak with a voice potential this very hour. They dogmatize to-day as imperiously as St. Hilaire, La Marck, Oken, Comte, or the author of the Vestiges. It is no small equipment, then, that is needed by the scholar, at the present time, and it is no little labor he is called upon to perform.

But in defending the truth, let us not suppose that all, our enemies have written or spoken, is false. We may learn wisdom, even from them. There is much they have wrought assiduously to furnish, which may be turned to good account in our cause. It is permitted to us, in the providence of God, to appropriate the learning, research, and oftentimes the arguments of the opposers of truth, and employ them for the overthrow of their false systems, as also for the establishment of the divine wisdom, power, and goodness. The foes of truth are made, in fact, the Gibeonites of the Camp of Isreal, sutlers and drudges, hewers of wood and drawers of water. Paul used Aratus, Menander, Epimenides, and Seneca. Solomon levied tribute from the Tyrians and Sidonians, when building the Temple. Moses enriched the Tabernacle with Egyptian gold. The "Ruins" and "Travels" of Volney are among the strongest evidence of Christianity. German exegesis and French explorations, furnish weapons of assault and defence to the friends of the Bible. Although the Philistine was struck to the ground by a pebble from the brook, yet his final decapitation was by means of his own sword. Thus it is that the defenders of truth are permitted, and even required, to use the very weapons brought into action by their enemies, and convert them into instruments of victory; and thus it is that laying hold of whatever is valuable in the research and learning of the age, we shall be able to add strength to our own cause, while at the same time we render useless to error the residuum of its unappropriated materials.

With such a purpose, then, let us go hopefully into the field of action. Though, for the present, the sky seems stormy and covered with cloudy portents, yet a bright future awaits us, beckoning us onward with joy. It lies, not far distant beyond us, flashing in its golden beauty, like the glittering sheen of a sun-lit sea. It is a reward, in perspective, reserved for those who are worthy of it. Like the palm-bearing vision revealed to the eye of John, this also is given, to inspire the battlers of to-day with courage and with hope. An illustrious series of years springs anew on the scroll of time.—The last age of prophecy has arrived. Another and a regenerated one approaches;—an age to whose immortal nature and advance the grey traditions of the East, the songs of Roman Sibyls, the poetry of Jewish Bards, the promises of Heaven, the earnest expectation of the human race, and the painful struggle of almost two thousand years, conspire to testify,—an age when the colossal empire of Falsehood and Distrust shall crumble into ruins before the omnipotence of Truth and Faith,—an age when Truth delivered from the dross, which now obscures its splendor, shall shine with an unwonted radiance and crown the world with an unwonted glory;—an age uprising in the pristine grandeur of a new-born Paradise, decked with ornaments of grace, robed in spotless purity, and fresh again in all the smiles of innocence and charms of youth.

Meanwhile, our duty is to battle with the foe. The bugle-note, the note that summons to the charge, already greets our ears, and to-day our common Mother, Spartan-like, speaks to us all, and says, "*Your shields, my children, or upon them!*" Again she sends us forth, augmented in our numbers, by another band of brothers, issuing from her honored halls. Again her common blessing falls upon our heads. Let us labor to be worthy of her generous care. Let us arm ourselves for the mighty moral and intellectual conflict of the times in which we live. Let us put on the panoply of a true scholarship, the power of a pure purpose, and the courage of an exalted faith. In the words, the final and impressive, of the first oration ever pronounced before the Alumni of the University, let me say and entreat: "*Aim at, and sustain the high dignity of the True Scholar. Profane not your talents,—pervert not your priveleges,—disappoint not the expectations that cluster around you!*"

www.ingramcontent.com/pod-product-compliance
Lightning Source LLC
LaVergne TN
LVHW011147110826
845150LV00008B/2556

* 9 7 8 1 4 1 8 1 9 1 7 0 2 *